The Best Clean Jokes

Volume 1

By Molly Applesauce

327 Entertainment © 2012

All Rights Reserved.

Why did the robber get caught?

He wasn't wearing his sneakers.

Why did the baker get evicted?

He wasn't making enough dough!

What did the salad say to the refrigerator?

Lettuce in!

Why was the painting released from jail?

Because he was framed.

Why did the cat get a $500 summons?

For littering.

Why was the car ashamed?

He had bad gas.

Why didn't the bunny like the diamond earrings?

It didn't have enough karats!

Why did the jungle cat get dumped?

He was a cheetah.

Why did everyone admire the pen?

He always did the write thing!

Why was the sticker angry?

He didn't like being labeled.

Why was little William afraid?

He heard the bill collector was in town.

What do you get when a clown farts in your face?

Laughing gas.

Where do lunatics ride their bikes?

On the psycho path.

Why didn't the man attend the funeral?

He wasn't a mourning person.

Did you hear about Thomas Corn?

He was promoted to colonel.

Why did the horseman sleep during the day?

He could only go out at knight!

Why couldn't the drummer be an archaeologist?

He couldn't read the cymbals!

Why did the cake taste like pollen?

He had too much flower.

Why did the sea captain buy a new boat?

He got it on sail!

Why did the pony get detention?

He was horsing around.

Why did the spider major in computer programming?

He made really good web-sites.

What did the doctor tell the overweight frog?

He couldn't eat any more butter-flies.

Why was the shampoo mad?

She didn't get to see her soaps.

What did the teacher give the sick French fry?

Catch-up packets.

What did the cloud wear to the prom?

A rainbow.

What do you call a snowman's son & daughter?

His chill-dren.

What do you call a Snowman with children?

An icemaker.

What did the accountant say to the tennis court?

What's your net worth?

What are horses' favorite fruits?

Strawberries.

How does a barrette surf?

On a clipboard.

How does the Devil travel?

In a hell-icopter.

Why can't the match have any friends?

He keeps burning bridges!

Why was the cucumber nervous?

He was in a real pickle!

Why wasn't the toilet hungry?

He had too many crunch bars!

Where did the bees go after their wedding?

Their honeymoon.

What's a mattress's favorite season?

Spring.

How do you get lime disease in space?

You get bit by a luna-tic!

Why do scissors make good boxers?

They have good uppercuts.

What do you call overbearing parents?

A teen-ager.

How does a guppy eat soup?

From a fish bowl.

Why couldn't Monday lose weight?

She had too many Sundaes.

Why couldn't Saturday lose weight?

She had too many Fry-days.

Why was the horse sad?

Because he didn't make the chorale.

What did W say when X dumped her?

Y?

Why did the man hate public speaking?

He didn't own a diction-ary.

How did the judges score the alligator's performance?

On a scale of 1-10.

Why did Mr. Dynamite buy a new house?

Business was booming.

Why couldn't the chicken play with the band?

Because he broke his drumsticks.

What do you call a chicken revolution?

A coop-d'état.

How did the tree get into an accident?

He didn't see the leaves turning.

Why did the planet go see the doctor?

His asteroids were killing him.

What do you call overworked poultry?

Fried chicken.

What do you call 20 kittens in an antique shop?

A catastrophe.

Why didn't the great white have any friends?

He was a lone shark.

What did one hamburger say to the other?

Nice to meat you.

Why did the clock ruin dinner?

He didn't have enough thyme.

Why was the comb sad?

His friend kept brushing him off.

Why did Frankenstein's mom put him to bed?

He seamed tired.

Where did the taffy stay on vacation?

A suite!

What kind of bagels do pilots prefer?

Plane ones.

What did the wind give his daughter for her 16th birthday?

An heir-loom.

Why was my mother's sister mad?

I tried to put her in the aunt farm!

Why did the radish get suspended?

He beet someone up.

Where did the piano go on vacation?

The Florida Keys.

Where do the unruly children sleep?

In punk beds.

Why was the pencil rushed to the hospital?

He had lead poisoning.

Why didn't the woman buy the belt?

It was a waist of money!

What did the ghost spend all his money on?

Booze.

What lives in the alphabet forest?

V-owls.

Why do grizzlies hate the hospital?

They can't bear the sight of blood.

How did the fisherman impress his friends?

He showed them his mussels.

What do dogs and remote controls have in common?

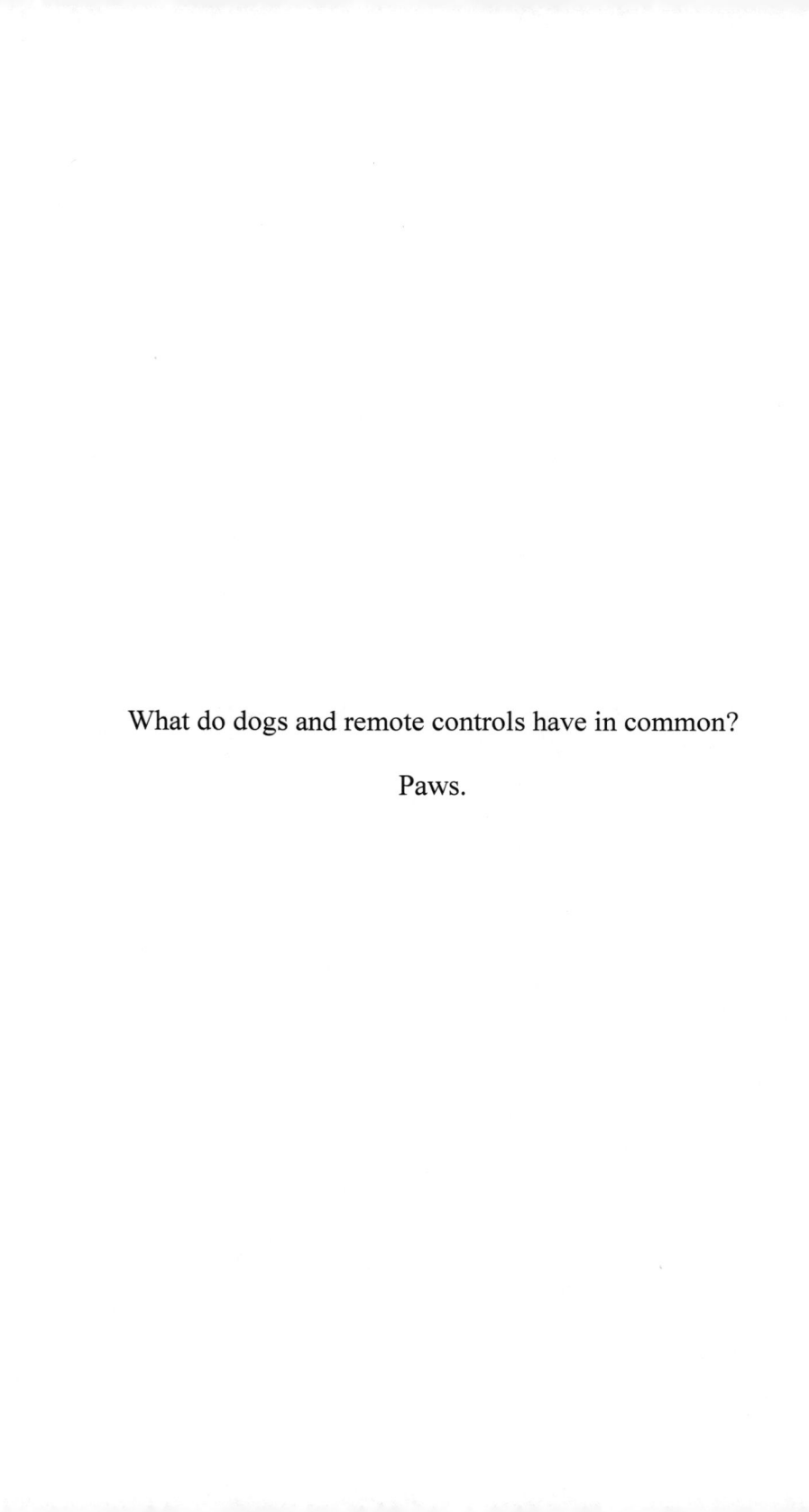

Paws.

Why do you call two curtains communicating?

A curtain call.

Why did the blanket hug the mattress?

To comfort-her.

Why did the AC call his friend?

He needed to vent.

Why didn't the book go the bar?

He didn't want to pay the cover.

Why did the voter leave the booth slowly?

He was watching out for the exit poll.

What do you call a man who repairs records?

A spin doctor.

Why was Mrs. Clause horrified?

She found Santa's slay.

Why did the tomato's parents disown him?

They found out he was a fruit!

What do you call a pig in a vice?

Pulled pork.

Why did the school nurse send the trashcan home?

He looked a little pale.

What did the number 3 do before dinner?

He set the multiplication table.

How did the goldsmith use the internet?

With his compewter.

Why didn't Melissa listen to "The Noggins?"

She hated headbands.

Where do cars take their children on Saturdays?

The park.

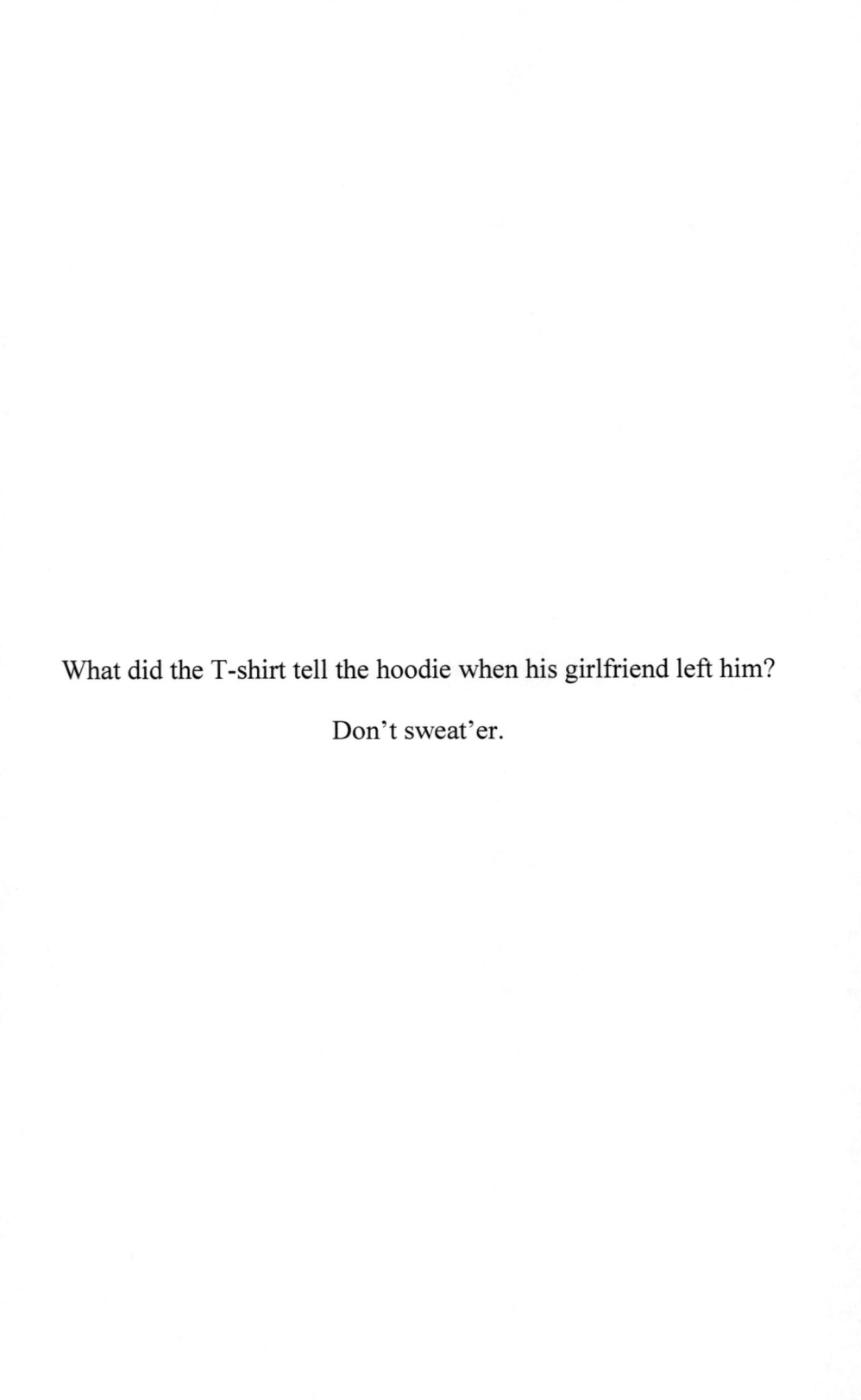

What did the T-shirt tell the hoodie when his girlfriend left him?

Don't sweat'er.

Where does yeast live?

In a high rise.

What do midgets wear during the summer?

Shorts.

How do dwarfs get through the work day?

They make small talk.

Where do the houses have more than 1 living room?

In Denmark.

Why did the shoe lace break up with his girlfriend?

He didn't want to string her along.

How did the cheese wedge get a math tutor?

He wasn't doing grate.

What did the slaves do on their day off?

Serf.

Why did the shoes go to heaven?

Because they had good souls.

Why did the doctor kill his wife?

Because he lost his patients.

Why was the grape grounded?

Because all he did was wine.

What do vampires hate to eat for dinner?

Steaks.

Why was the Sun angry?

The sky raised his rent!

What did the number 6 do at 7?

He eight!

What does a vulture do on Sundays?

He preys.

What did the chromosome wear to school?

Blue genes.

Why didn't the violin like the tuba?

She thought he was too brass.

What happens when the Sun gets angry?

He throws a temperature tantrum.

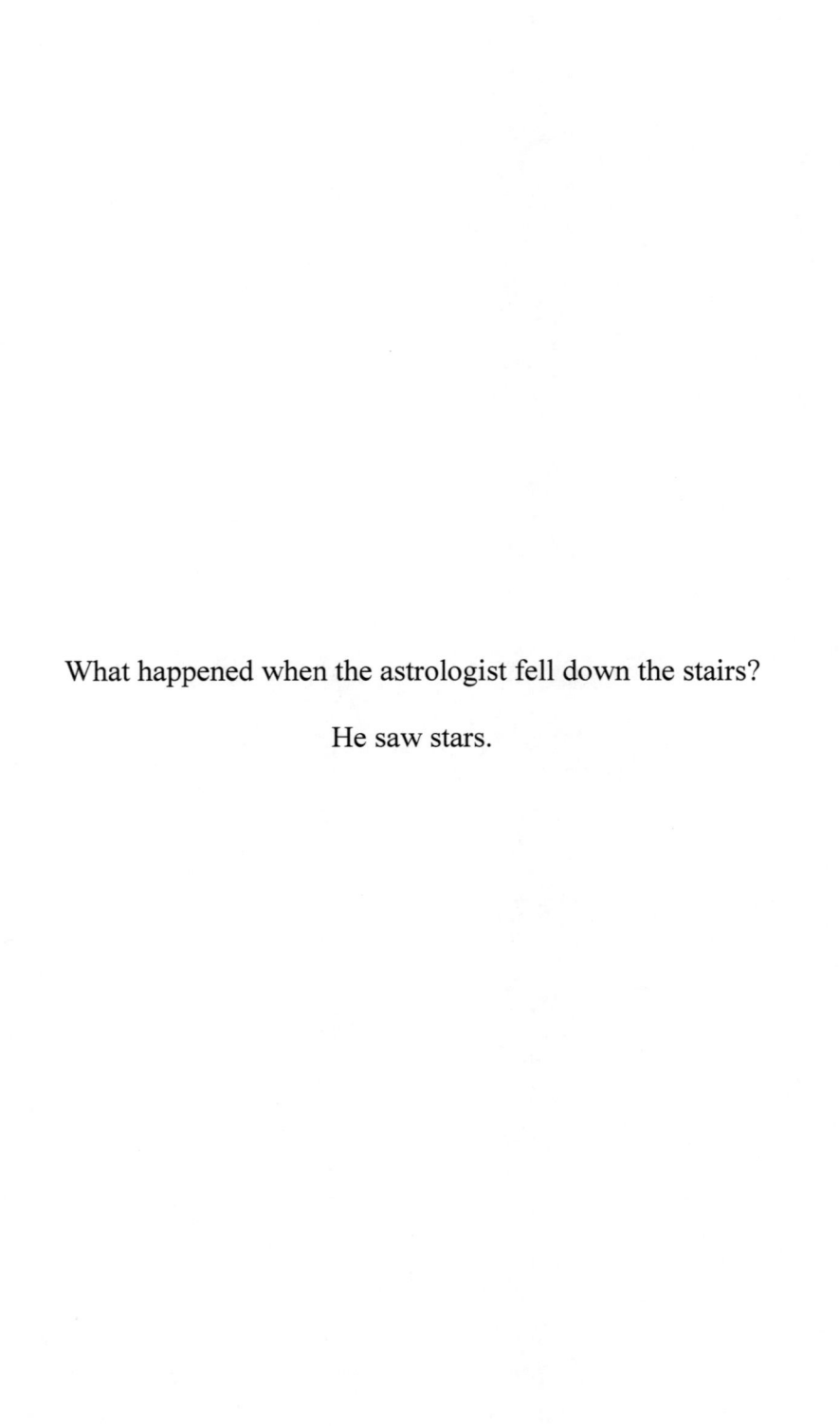

What happened when the astrologist fell down the stairs?

He saw stars.

What do fish hate most of all?

Tank tops.

What do you call notebooks sitting in traffic?

A paper jam.

What did the sedan buy his wife for Valentines Day?

A carnation.

How do you know a necktie is hungry?

He scarfs his food down.

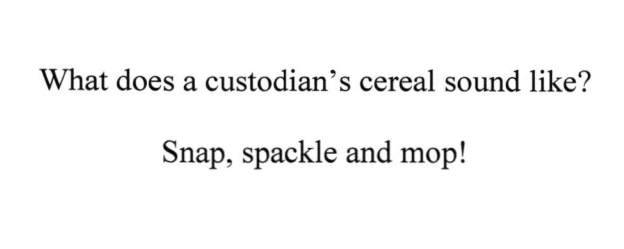

What does a custodian's cereal sound like?

Snap, spackle and mop!

Why was the door mat crying?

People kept stepping on him.

Why did the skeleton call his friend?

He had a bone to pick with him!

What is a fireplace's favorite card game?

Poker.

Why did the anvil cry himself to sleep?

He had a heavy heart.

Why do people hate flip flops?

They always change their minds.

What do you call a piece of paper that doesn't exercise?

Stationary.

What do you call a potato in a pool float?

A tuber.

Why did the rams get into a fight?

One kept goating the other.

How does a computer eat?

In mega-bytes.

Why didn't the soda have any money?

He got canned.

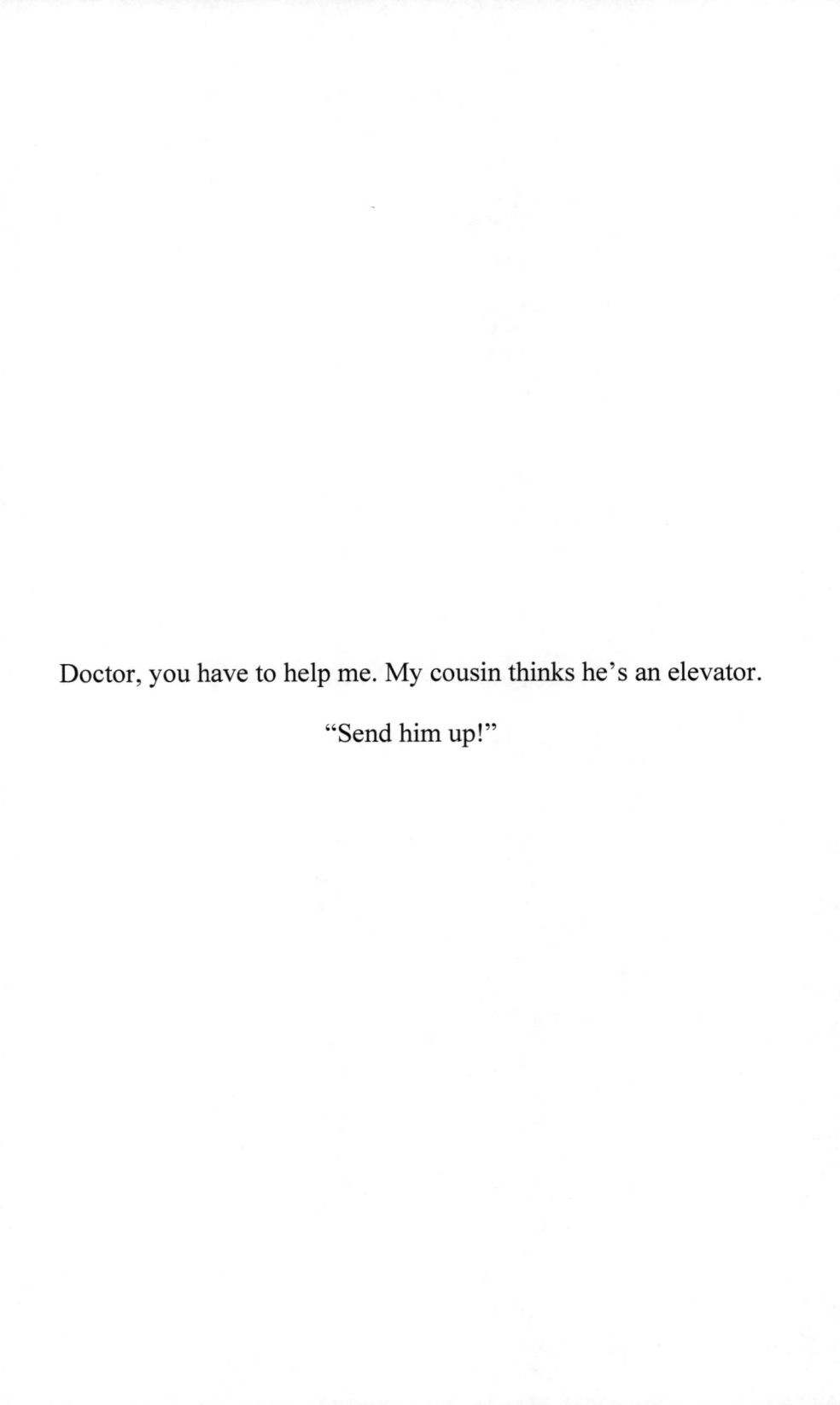

Doctor, you have to help me. My cousin thinks he's an elevator.

"Send him up!"

Why did the scissor get thrown out of the movie theater?

He kept cutting the lines.

What do bakers wear on their feet?

Loafers.

What do you wear when you sprain your wrist?

A brace-let.

What do you call a city dweller in space?

A cosmopolitan.

Why did the hammer get the lead in the school play?

He nailed the audition.

What do you call a man who fears spaceships?

An astro-not.

Why did the pin pay cash?

He didn't want to pay the tacks.

Why did the cantaloupe start crying?

He was melon-choly.

Why did the farmer buy more soil?

It was dirt cheap.

How did the pillar earn a living?

She was a columnist.

Where can you read boring articles?

In a snooze-paper.

Why was the dresser embarrassed?

He lost his drawers.

How many cars do most priests have?

Nun.

Why did they close the library?

It was overrun with bookworms.

What instrument do fish play well?

The bass guitar.

What do you call a toucan who robs a bank?

A jailbird.

Why was the bear sad?

Because he missed his honey.

What do you call a dog in an SUV?

A carpet.

What do selfish people get?

The measles.

How did the gourd react to being fired?

It squashed him.

What did the lawyer wear to bed each night?

A retainer.

Why were the fish's parents displeased?

Their son got kicked out of the school.

Where do homes buy their groceries?

The housing market.

What do steel workers listen to?

Heavy metal.

What's the most valuable flower?

A marigold.

Why do people respect straws?

They tend to be suck-sesful.

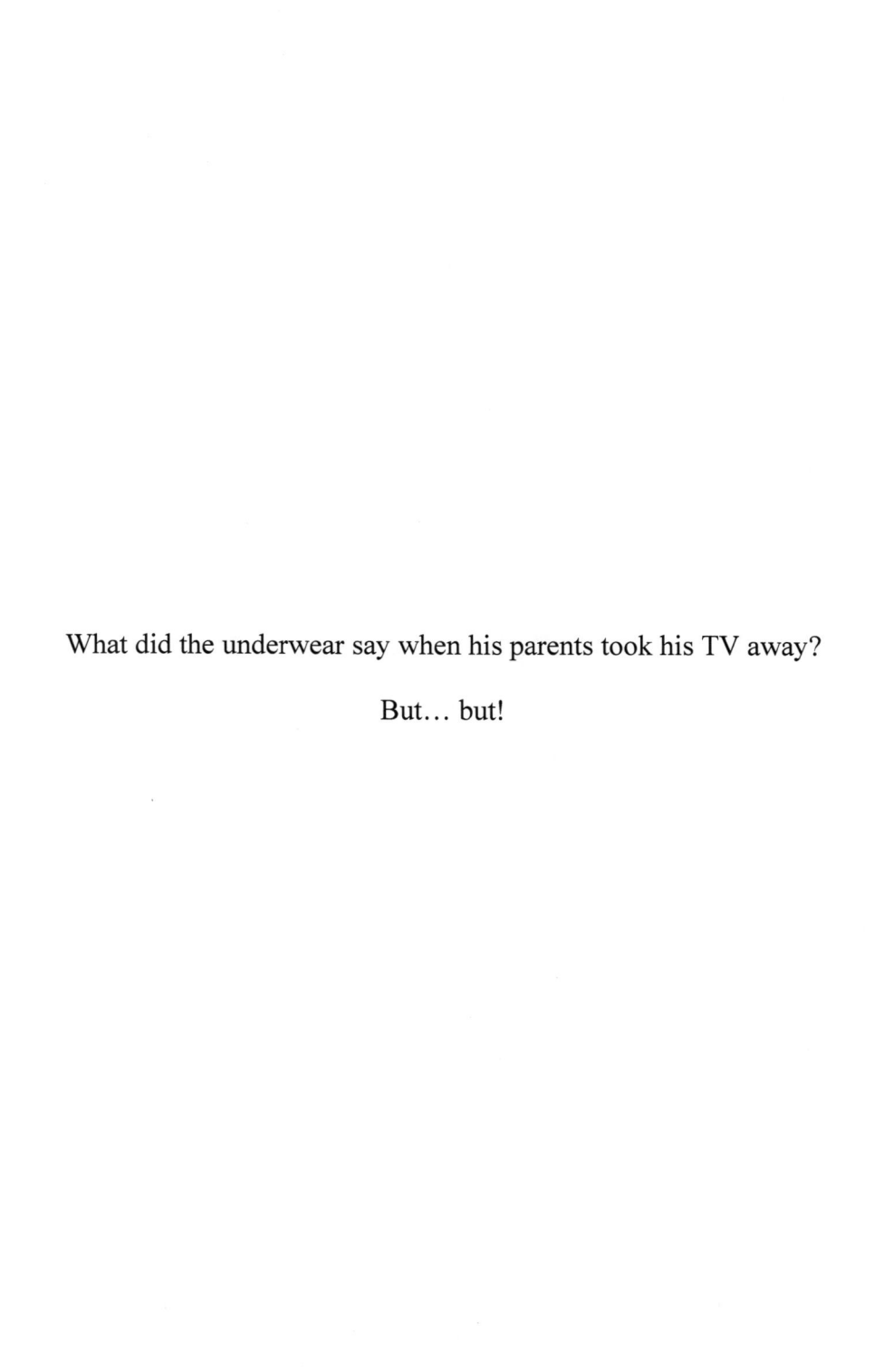

What did the underwear say when his parents took his TV away?

But... but!

Why couldn't the clock play in the baseball game?

He forgot his gear.

Why did the seaweed get a tutor?

He needed kelp with his homework.

Why didn't the cows speak to one another?

They had beef.

Why did the farmer get rid of his chickens?

He bought eggplants instead.

Why did the driver put on a bathing suit?

Because she was carpooling.

What do beggars eat for breakfast?

Poorage.

How do you renovate an auditorium?

In stages.

What does the devil put in his hot cocoa?

Sinamin.

Why did the teacher yell at the bike wheel?

He spoke out of turn.

Why didn't Cain come to the party?

He wasn't Abel.

What do you call a horse that can't sleep?

A nightmare.

Where do flashlights hang out?

Battery Park.

Why did the mouse get kicked out of the FBI?

They thought he was a rat.

Where does the flu go on vacation?

Germ-any.

Why did the mic walk off the stage?

He couldn't stand the singer.

What does the rifle use after a shower?

Gunpowder.

Where do textbooks sleep?

Nap sacks.

What's an elk's favorite dessert?

Chocolate mouse.

Why did the novel start wearing high heels?

She was tired of being a short story.

Why did the kangaroo call the police?

Somebody stole his pouch.

Why didn't the dentist give Charles any novocain?

He'd turn into a numb Chuck.

Why did the ship have a nervous breakdown?

He was a wreck.

Why do clouds wear Band-Aid's?

Because of the skyscrapers.

What does a sneaker where to her wedding?

Shoelace.

Why was the Earth hard to live with?

It's bipolar.

Why were the stairs unhappy?

Because they didn't like their stepmom.

What do hogs read to their children?

Pigtails.

Why did the steam boat try to fly?

He heard about the new airport.

What kind of music to garden flowers listen to?

Bedrock.

What do you call a man who can't keep a girlfriend?

A ladybug.

What do you get when you cross a bunny and a church?

A bellhop.

Why do vampires hate volleyball?

The spiking.

What do you call a watch with no common sense?

Counterclockwise.

Why couldn't the man turn his steering wheel?

He was a backseat driver.

Where can people of all races, ages and creeds drink water?

A farewell.

What lives in a forest and is always jealous?

An evergreen.

What do armchairs say when they stub their toes?

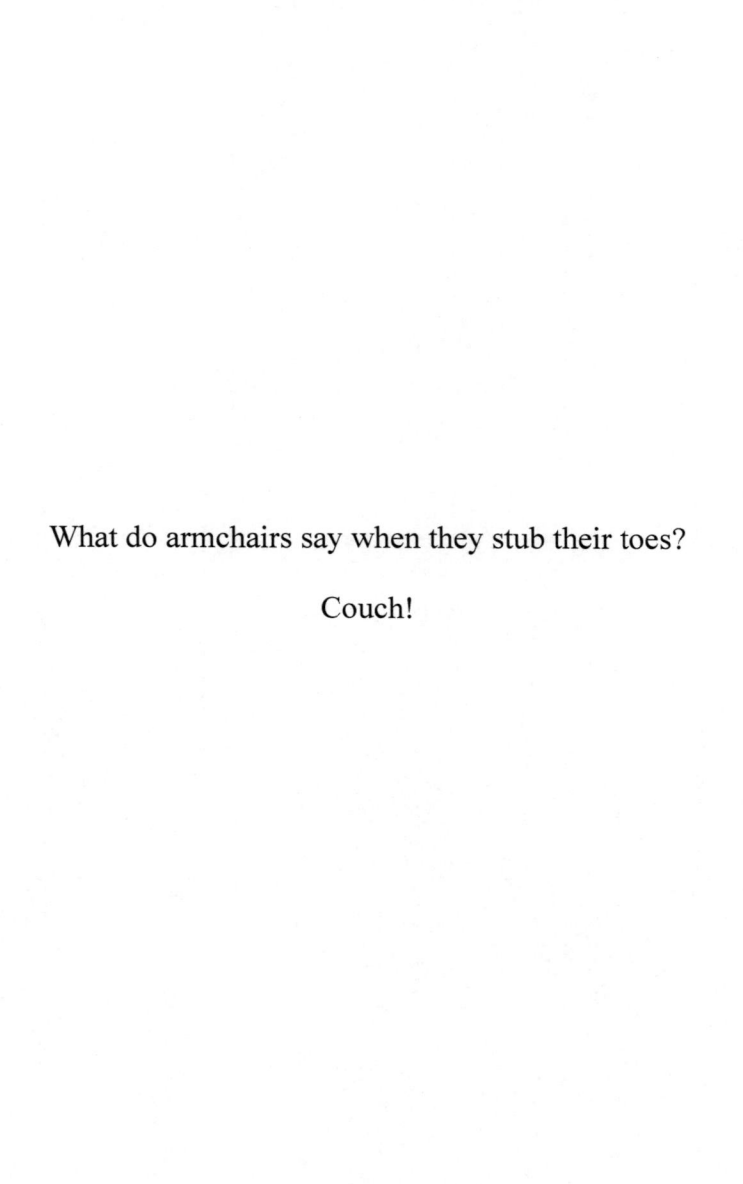

Couch!

What do pitchers keep on their beds?

Throw pillows.

What do knives use when gambling?

Dice.

Why does a burrito never call you back?

He's always wrapped up.

Why was the banana depressed?

He and his wife split.

Why did the dog ignore the vet's phone calls?

He didn't want the de-tails.

Why did the cemetery caretaker stay home from work?

He was gravely ill.

Why did the cooks get thrown out of the party?

They kept stirring the pot!

Where do towels go during the summer?

The bleach!

Why were the eyeglasses embarrassed?

They made a spectacle of themselves.

What do you get when you cross a toolbox with a chimp?

A monkey wrench.

Why do maids hate churches?

There's so much stained glass!

What kind of dogs do football players love?

Golden receivers.

Did you hear about the cow that tried to ride a skateboard?

It was an udder disaster!

What's a toilet's favorite instrument?

The pee-ano.

How does an Ox write letters?

With a bullpen.

Why did the soda lose the singing competition?

He was flat.

What do octopuses bring on camping trips?

Their tent-acles.

One did the cactus promise his girlfriend?

That he'd never desert her.

What did Jack Frost say to his neighbor?

Have an ice weekend!

What kinds of snakes make excellent conductors?

Copperheads.

Why didn't Tuesday go to the gym?

He was feeling week.

How do archers get in line?

In arrow.

Why couldn't the seashell get out of bed?

He kept getting hit with waves of depression.

Where do swimmers go after work?

A dive bar.

Why wasn't the zombie invited to the party?

He was a real stiff!

Why did the brain run to the station?

He didn't want to miss his train of thought.

What do you call an angel who wears perfume?

Heaven scent.

What do you get when you cross a haunted house with a river?

A creeking door.

Why did the raspberry and blueberry stop fighting?

They decided to berry the hatchet.

Why didn't the tree's friends ask him to buy liquor?

They knew he woodn't do it.

Why didn't the sheet attend the meeting?

He had more pressing matters to attend to.

Why don't churches make any money?

They're a non-prophet organization.

What do you call a shoe that invents things?

Patent leather.

How did the shepherd get out of trouble?

He found a scapegoat.

Why do poor people love the desert?

The unlimited sandwiches.

What do you call a pig with big dreams?

A porkupine.

How do witches stay in shape?

They hexercise.

What does every weeping willow own?

A bolling bawl.

How do clothing stores make money?

They invest.

Why did the employees feel awkward?

They didn't like their boss' crew-cut.

What do most hip hop artists carry with them?

Rap sheets.

What did one mechanic say to the other?

Give me a brake!

Did you hear about the puzzle who fell in love?

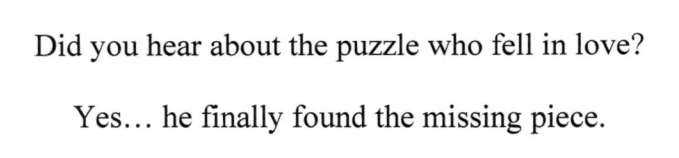

Yes… he finally found the missing piece.

What does a chocolate bar do when you tell him a joke?

He snickers.

What do you call clothing that plays instruments?

An ensemble.

Why did the pony cancel her performances?

She was a little hoarse.

Why did the government ban the movie?

The special effects were breathtaking.

What do you call a mountain with the stomach virus?

A volcano.

What do power plants do when they're unhappy?

They revolt.

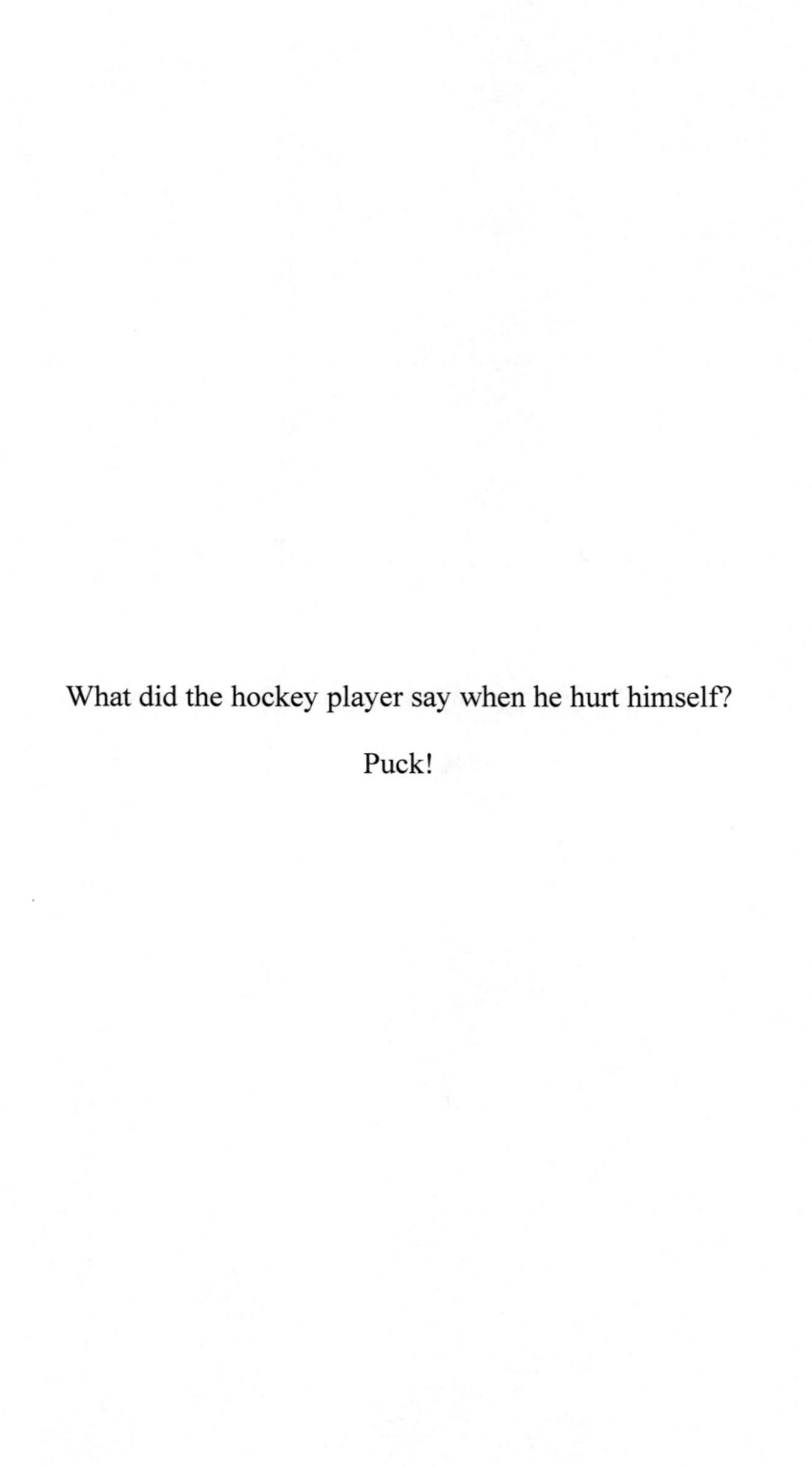

What did the hockey player say when he hurt himself?

Puck!

Why did the author wear make up?

She hated her preface.

Why did the math textbook see a shrink?

He had so many problems.

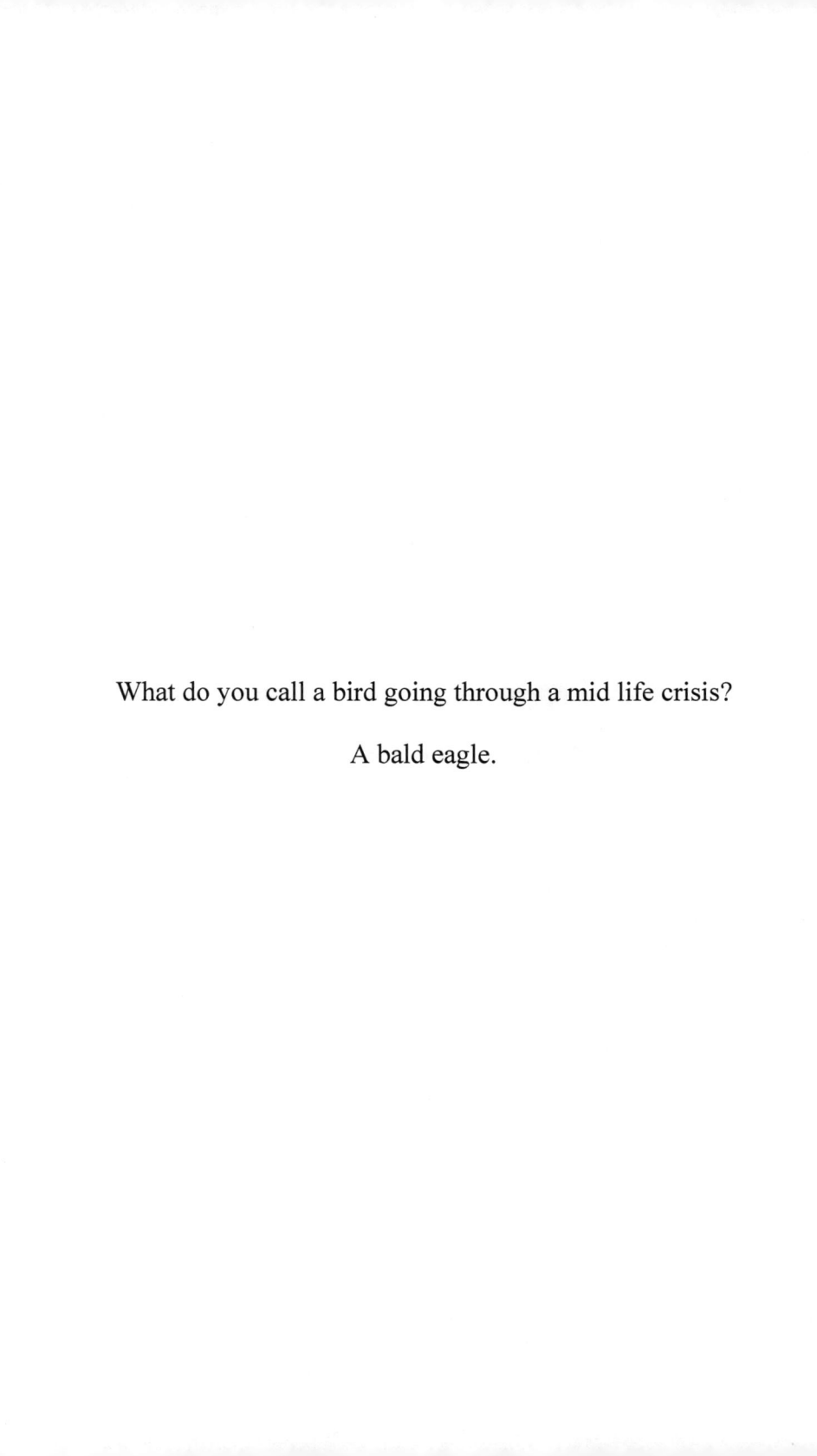

What do you call a bird going through a mid life crisis?

A bald eagle.

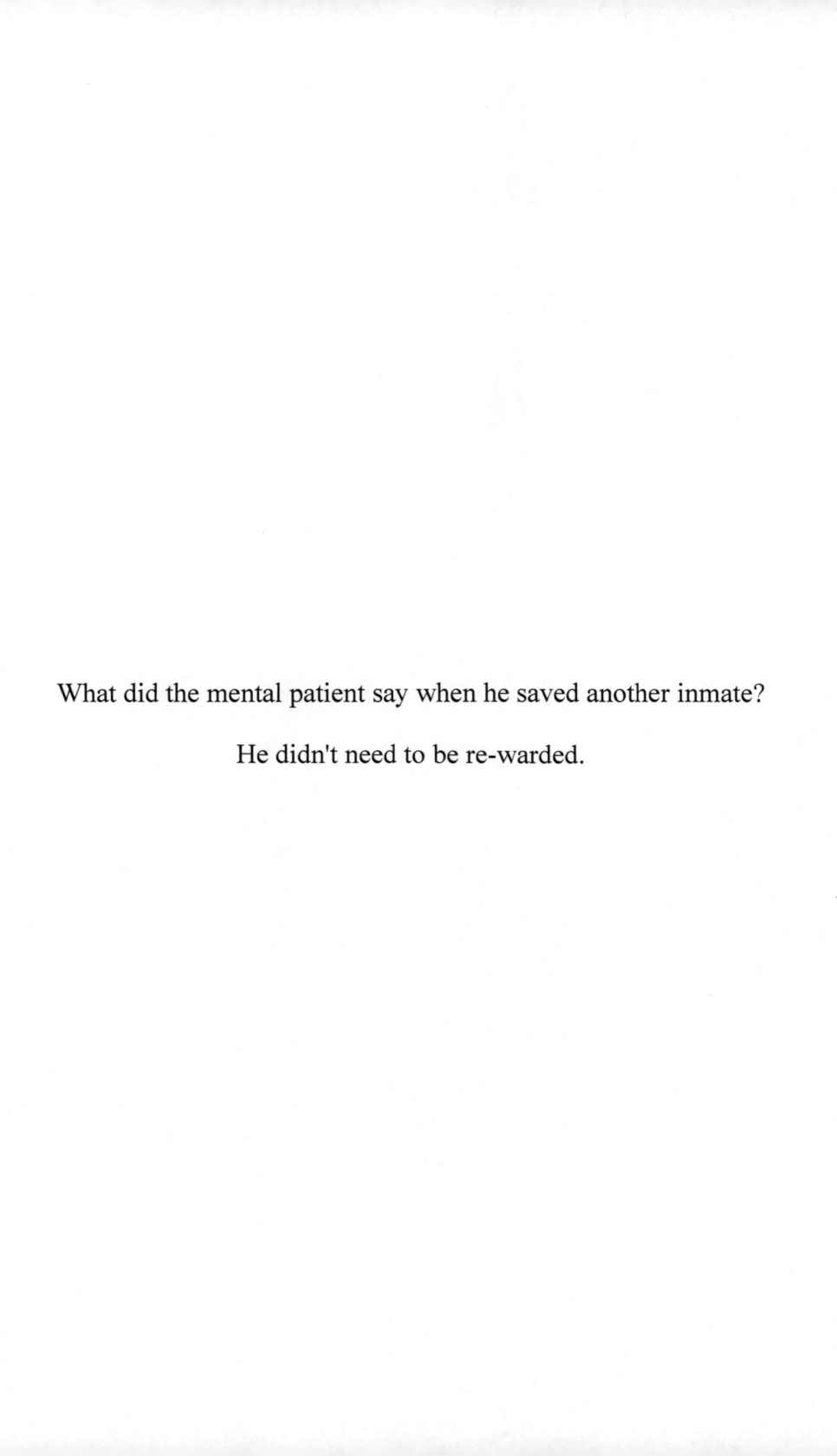

What did the mental patient say when he saved another inmate?

He didn't need to be re-warded.

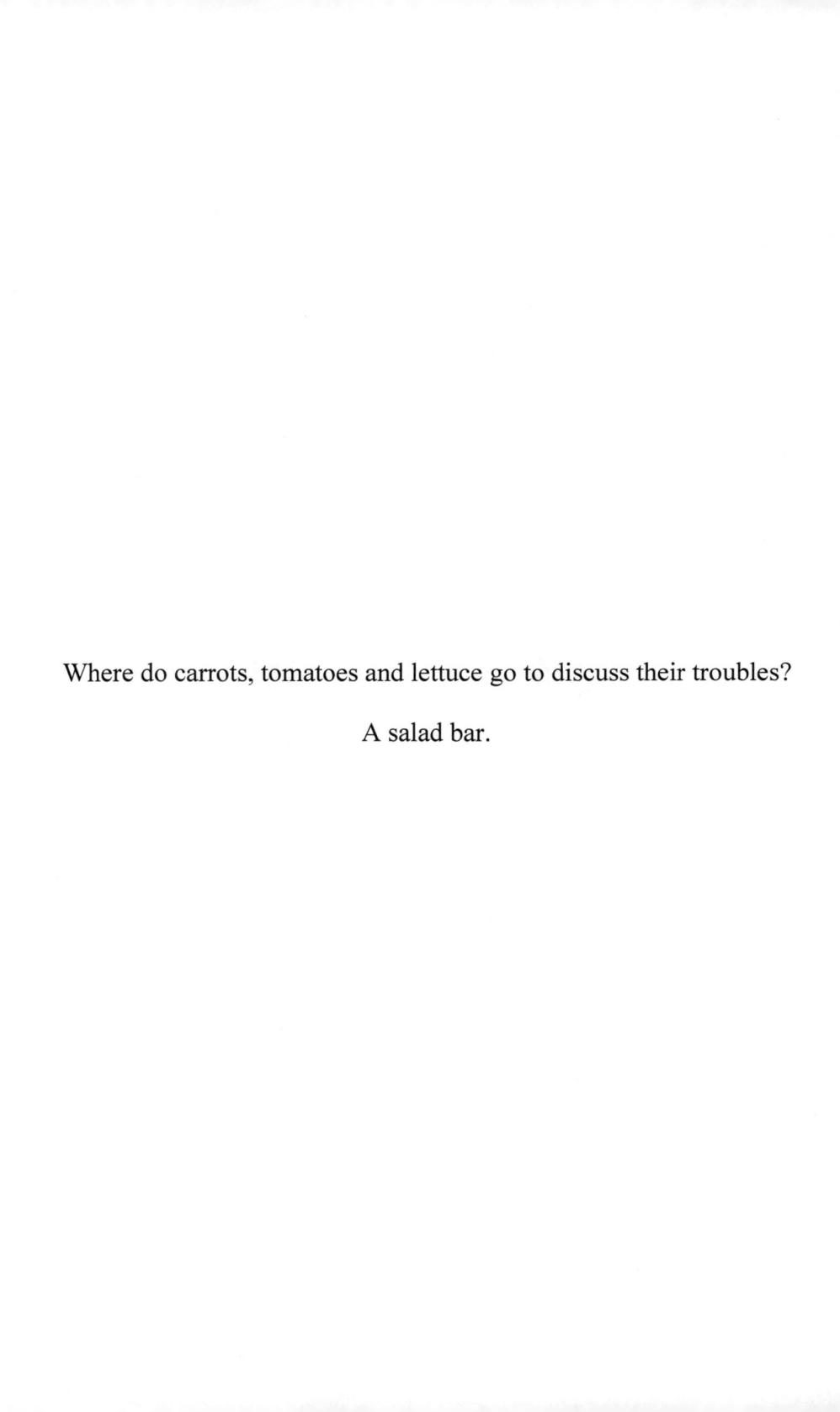

Where do carrots, tomatoes and lettuce go to discuss their troubles?

A salad bar.

Why do people call Detroit the windy city?

Because the people there love chili.

Why was the man banned from the supermarket?

He was a known cereal killer.

Why did Arty get boo-ed off the stage?

He choked!

What do rich sheep drive?

Lamborghinis.

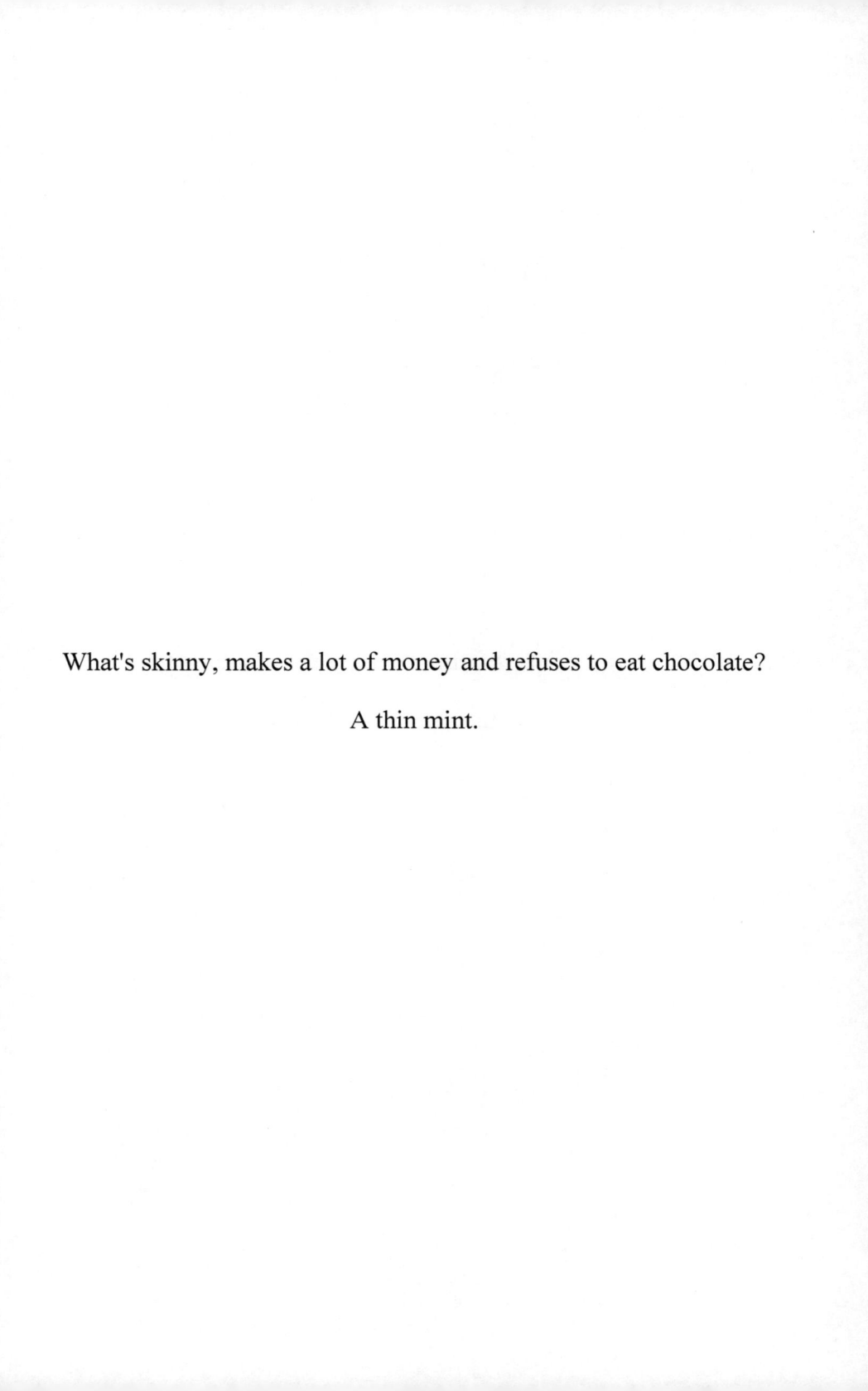

What's skinny, makes a lot of money and refuses to eat chocolate?

A thin mint.

Why was the fruit fired from the fruit stand?

He kept hitting the applesauce.

Why are mushrooms always so happy?

They have lots of fungus.

What's a burglar's favorite hairstyle?

Dreadlocks.

What do English teachers eat for snack?

Grammar crackers.

Why did the chicken get detention?

He was using fowl language in class.

Where do trout keep their money?

A river bank.

What do shoes use to build their houses?

Sandalwood.

Why did the US soccer team return their uniforms?

The New Jersey-s smelt bad.

Why don't you ever see trees on Jeopardy?

They're easily stumped.

Why did the king go to the dentist?

He needed a new crown.

Why is Jesus afraid of the city?

He heard about the crosswalks.

How do pirates do their food shopping?

They go isle by isle.

Why did the T shirt feel sad?

Because his cousin dyed.

Why couldn't the priest wear his new robe?

It needed to be altared.

Why did the lemon feel depressed?

He lost his zest for life.

Why was the menopausal teacher happy?
She only had one more period left!

Printed in Great Britain
by Amazon